A CHRISTMAS BOOK

FOR THE

UKULELE BEGINNER

Faye Hicks

Also by Faye Hicks:
Defining Moments
A Day in the Life of a Professor
Who Says You Can't Herd Cats?

Read more about (and by) Faye Hicks at these sites:
www.fayehicks.com
fayehicks.wordpress.com

DEDICATION

To Sylvia – my ukulele buddy!

Authors Notes

A couple of years ago I bought a ukulele. I'd been playing guitar in a little band with three other guitarists and I wanted to add something a bit more unique to our sound. I had originally thought about trying to learn the mandolin, but after checking that out I found it to be too hard on the fingers and way too much to learn. So I decided to try a ukulele… It turned out to be a super decision – I don't think you will find an instrument that is easier to play and yet it offers such a wide variety of sounds. Strum it quickly and get a mandolin/banjo kind of sound; strum each string slowly and deliberately and it sounds almost like a harp, pick individual strings and get the true Hawaiian ukulele sound.

When I first thought about getting a ukulele I had so many questions: what size should I buy, what brand(s) should I look for, and which tuning should I choose? Then once I got my ukulele, I again had a ton of questions: what are the finger positions for the various chords, should I strum it or pick each string individually, and how can I become proficient as quickly as possible? In the end I spent a lot of time researching information and even more time figuring things out for myself. My idea in writing this book is to save you some time by answering these same questions for you.

This book is aimed at the complete beginner and can be used in a couple of ways. For the parent looking to get their son or daughter a ukulele, this book first provides advice on what to look for when choosing a ukulele. This book can then be given as a Christmas gift (along with the ukulele) to provide some basic instructions and songs to get them started. If you're planning to buy your own ukulele, you can read the advice provided in this book directly and, once you have your ukulele, you'll also be able to use this book to get started playing Christmas tunes right away.

Whatever your approach, I hope you enjoy this wonderful instrument! Happy holidays!

Faye Hicks
December 2012

Table of Contents

Introduction

Ukuleles have become very popular recently and no wonder. They're a small and lightweight instrument and therefore extremely portable. Whether you're hopping a bus across town or taking a plane cross-country – you can easily carry your ukulele right along with you. It's also very easy to learn to play a ukulele. Unlike mandolin and guitar chords, which can get pretty difficult, most of the basic ukulele chords are really easy to play, requiring only 2 or 3 fingers. As a result, it doesn't take long to learn a few songs on your ukulele. You can get a pretty good range of sounds out of a good ukulele, as well – depending upon whether you strum all the strings at once or pick each string individually. A ukulele is a particularly terrific first instrument for a child, or for any one taking up a musical instrument for the first time, because of its small size, soft (nylon) strings, and easy chords.

This book is aimed at the complete beginner – especially those who have never played a fretted stringed instrument before. I'll start with advice on buying your first ukulele and I'll also describe the essential accessories. Then I'll provide some basic instructions on how to get started playing your new ukulele. I've also included some Christmas song sheets to get you going this festive season. So let's get started!

Advice on Buying a Ukulele

The first thing to decide when buying a ukulele is what size you want. Ukuleles come in four sizes: the 'soprano' is the smallest, the next size up is a 'concert' ukulele, then the 'tenor' and finally the largest is the 'baritone'. If you're interested in the actual dimensions for each, there's a handy chart below (data source: *www.ukuleleworld.com*). The three smallest sizes: soprano, concert and tenor, all have the same tuning – so the chords are the same on all three. Learn to play any one of these and you can pick up either of the other two and start playing immediately. The baritone is the exception – it has the same setup as the highest four strings on a standard six-string guitar – and that's totally different from the three smaller ukuleles.

Ukulele Dimensions (in inches)				
Type	Soprano	Concert	Tenor	Baritone
Total Length	$21\,^1/_{16}$	$23\,^1/_4$	$26\,^1/_4$	$30\,^{11}/_{16}$
Body Length	$9\,^1/_2$	11	$12\,^1/_{16}$	14
Scale Length	$13\,^5/_8$	$14\,^3/_4$	17	$20\,^1/_8$

So – which size to buy? Well if you are buying for a small child, a soprano ukulele might be a good idea since it's ideally suited to small hands and fingers. However, I think that most older children, teens, and adults will find the fingerboard on a concert or tenor sized ukulele a bit less cramped. You'll also get a nicer sound out of the larger ukuleles. My sister-in-law has a concert sized ukulele and it definitely has a lovely sound, but I do find the frets a bit too closely spaced for my chubby fingers. I have a tenor ukulele (shown here on the left) and I find it's perfect! If you already play the guitar and you're just looking for something more portable for those times when you don't want to lug around a full sized guitar, then maybe the baritone is for you, since there will be no new chords to learn.

My tenor ukulele shown here next to a guitar for size comparison.

Next, the question is: what brand to buy and how much money to spend? Here, the important thing to remember is to keep away from the "toys". They are difficult to tune, have a crappy sound and are generally very frustrating to play. Last year I took some ukulele lessons on a cruise to Hawaii and our instructor had a great buying tip. He told us *"if a ukulele is a pretty color, or if it has any words or scenery painted on it – chances are it's a toy, not an instrument."* These are attractively priced ukuleles (usually $15 to $50) and they make wonderful souvenirs – but they can be extremely difficult to keep in tune. In the end, all you'll ever get to play on it will be your hit single *"Tune Up"*. Very frustrating! While steering clear of the painted ukuleles, here are three other things for you to consider carefully: the tuning method, the material the ukulele is made of, and the way the strings are attached.

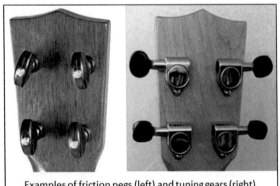

Examples of friction pegs (left) and tuning gears (right).

When I say the tuning method, I mean the mechanism for tightening the strings. This can be done either by using friction pegs (little pegs that you twist), or by using tuning gears as you typically see on a guitar. Examples of both are shown on the left. The tuning gears are usually covered with little metal cases; the photo on the right shows what the actual gears look like inside.

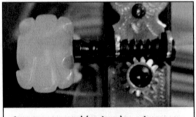

An uncovered (guitar) tuning gear.

Some ukulele purists may swear by friction pegs – mainly for authenticity – and some of the most expensive instruments do have friction pegs (as do most of the cheap ones). However, in my opinion, geared tuning is the only way to go – friction pegs are very difficult to adjust precisely and are highly prone to slipping. Even if you are buying a first instrument for a child; in fact, *especially* if you are buying a first instrument for a child, make sure you avoid friction pegs for tuning – they will lead to endless frustration.

In terms of the material the ukulele is made of, I am not actually talking about the type of wood – although to many people that is a big factor in choosing a ukulele. I'm referring to the choice between laminated wood (plywood) and solid wood. Generally solid wood instruments are very expensive and sound amazing, whereas laminated wood instruments are relatively inexpensive and don't sound quite as nice. There are some laminated wood instruments out there that do have a fairly decent sound, but just listen to one alongside a solid wood instrument and

My ukulele has a solid spruce top and laminated wood sides and back – it has a beautiful rich sound!

you'll quickly hear what I mean. Assuming that you are not a professional musician who needs (and can afford) instruments that cost thousands of dollars – you're likely not going to want to pay big bucks for a solid wood ukulele. Fortunately, there's an economical compromise. Look for an instrument with a solid wood top and laminated wood sides and back. It's the vibration of the top that has the most influence on the sound, so having the top made of solid wood at least, will give you a huge improvement in sound for only a marginal increase in cost.

Next, pay special attention to how the strings are attached at the bridge. This may seem like a small issue – but I've found that if they're just held in place by a little knot at the end of a slit, they tend to slip out too easily, especially as the slits get worn. Instead, you want to be able to loop the strings right through and tie them to get a good tight grip (as shown here in the photo on the left).

Finally, the biggest question… What brand to buy? My best advice on this is to try out as many ukuleles as possible before making your final choice. Obviously this means that you should not buy one online or by mail-order. The first test any ukulele must pass, in my opinion, is whether it can hold a tune. So when you go to buy your ukulele, go to a music store and ask the salesperson to show you how to tune it. Then test every ukulele in the shop and tune each one before you try it. Find one that is easy to tune, that is gentle on the fingers, and which sounds sweet when you gently strum the strings. If you know someone who plays the ukulele, ask them to come to the shop with you and get them to play them all for you. It really helps you to decide which one(s) you like the sound of best if you can hear some real music played on them. They can also give you some feedback on how easy they are to tune and how comfortable they are to play. If you don't know anyone who plays, then you can always ask the salesperson to play them for you. Don't be embarrassed to ask this, they will smell a sale and will be happy to do it. If none of the sales staff can play the ukuleles for you, this should be a clue for you to try a different store.

It's definitely important to make sure that the ukulele is not too hard on your chording fingers. However, comfort issues for the chording hand can be something you don't get a good feel for until you've been playing your ukulele for a while. Problems usually occur because the nut is a bit too high, which lifts the strings too far off the fingerboard. As a result you need to press really hard to get a decent sound out of it, which is hard on your 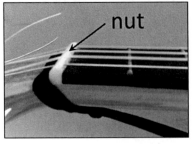 fingers. Most stock instruments need a bit of nut adjustment, so be sure to get a promise to include any required adjustments in the price before you shell out your hard earned cash. Any reputable music shop will be more than happy to do this for you, although they generally put a time limit of 1 to 3 months on it.

My tenor ukulele has lots of room for my chubby fingers.

So how much should you expect to pay for all of these features that I am suggesting? In western Canada it will likely cost you something in the range of $175 to $300. If you opt for laminate wood instead of solid wood for the top, you can probably get a decent ukulele for $80 to $150. Prices seem to be comparable in Hawaii and perhaps a little less expensive in the continental USA. I tried a lot of makes and models before settling on my first ukulele, and ended up buying a tenor Kala, with a solid spruce top and laminated wood sides and back, for about $300. I tried some very nice concert sized Kalas at about $175 as well, but chose the more expensive tenor model because it was more comfortable to play (because it has more space between the frets) and it came with a built in pickup which I needed for performing.

If the person who will be playing this ukulele is left-handed, you're naturally wondering by now if you can (or should) be buying them a left-handed ukulele. I'm left-handed too, so I face this

4

question whenever I learn any new instrument. When I was a small child, I used to pick up my brother's guitar (whenever he wasn't looking) and I'd always want to hold it backwards so I could strum with my left hand. It just 'felt' more natural. However, a few years later when I started taking guitar lessons, my music teacher convinced me to at least try to play 'right-handed' for a little while before giving in to the urge to do it 'backwards'. He had a few good reasons that convinced me to give 'right-handed' playing a try:

1. Musical instruments are built to be strung in a certain way; that is, they can't just be strung backwards if you hope to get optimal sound out if them. In fact, in some cases, you can actually damage the instrument by stringing it backwards. True 'left-handed' instruments are difficult to find and are usually much more expensive.

2. All of the chord charts are presented for right handed play; you'd have to figure out mirror images of all of them to be able to play left-handed.

3. Playing guitar (or ukulele) is a *two-handed* job and both hands have equally complicated tasks to learn – it's not like one hand has an easier job anyway.

When I started playing, it actually felt equally awkward either way, so it didn't really matter a lot which I chose. Given that fact, I decided it would be less complicated to just play right-handed. Once I got into it and began learning the more difficult chords, I realized that I actually had a bit of an advantage over the typical right-hander, since my (dominant) left hand is stronger and more nimble anyway. I also found that I learned more quickly, since I could mimic my instructor directly instead of having to figure out a mirror image of everything.

So, my advice to the other left-handers out there is that it's actually not any harder to learn to play right-handed, and it's certainly less complicated in terms of figuring out the chord charts. So why not at least give right-handed play a try? If you're determined to play left-handed, the good news is that your ukulele isn't likely to be damaged by stringing it backwards, since all the strings are just nylon (not steel) and they're not remarkably different in thickness. In terms of sound quality, it might make a difference for very expensive ukuleles but I doubt that it matters much for the typical beginner's ukulele. So, in the end, if you do decide to play left-handed, I don't think you need to buy a special ukulele for it.

Essential Accessories

Before you leave the store there are a few more essential items that you will need for your ukulele: a tuner, a shoulder strap, and a case.

The tuner:

You absolutely must tune your ukulele each and every time you play, *before* you start playing. It doesn't matter if you are going to play for a minute or an hour – you'll never develop an ear for music if you don't tune your instrument every single time you pick it up. Therefore, unless you are an unusually gifted musician, you're going to need an electronic tuner. You can get free "apps" for your smartphone that do this, you can use free tuners online, or you can buy an electronic tuner at the music shop. Do yourself (and your family) a huge favor – get your tuner as soon as you get your ukulele, and use it religiously. I opted to get one that clips right on my ukulele – that way it's always handy and, as a result, I can be tuned and ready to play in less than 10 seconds. This one cost about $30.

The shoulder strap:

Most ukuleles do not have a button on them to attach a strap – but you can add this for less than 5 bucks at most reputable music shops *(that is, ones that have a qualified luthier on staff to service, repair, and adjust stringed instruments)*, and this will enable you to put a little mandolin strap on your ukulele. *(Note – adding a button may void your warranty; fortunately there are also straps made specifically for ukuleles that just clip onto the sound*

hole.) The advantage of adding a shoulder strap is that it means your left hand is free to worry

only about chording – not supporting – the fingerboard, so you will be able to change chords much more easily (and eventually, much more quickly). It also means that your right hand/arm is free to pick or strum so you will be able to try more patterns and do them with greater ease. Even if you always sit to play, I think you will find that a shoulder strap will rocket you up the learning curve.

The case:

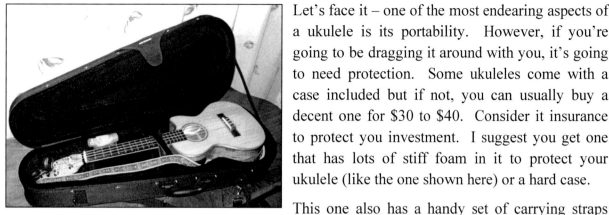

Let's face it – one of the most endearing aspects of a ukulele is its portability. However, if you're going to be dragging it around with you, it's going to need protection. Some ukuleles come with a case included but if not, you can usually buy a decent one for $30 to $40. Consider it insurance to protect you investment. I suggest you get one that has lots of stiff foam in it to protect your ukulele (like the one shown here) or a hard case.

This one also has a handy set of carrying straps and plenty of room for my ukulele, the tuner, and even a little compartment for spare strings, picks, and other small items. You'll also see a little brown fabric bottle in there – that holds water to help keep the humidity at optimal levels inside the case. If you live in a dry climate like I do, a case with a humidifier is essential or your ukulele will crack and be ruined. Of course this means you have to keep the ukulele in the case whenever you're not using it (and the little bottle full of water).

Be aware that your case will not protect your ukulele against all perils. For example, you should never leave your ukulele in the car. In warm weather the heat builds up (even in the trunk) and this can actually melt the glue holding the ukulele together. In severe cold weather, contraction of the wood can lead to cracking. A good rule of thumb is that if you would be uncomfortable, so would your ukulele.

Playing Your Ukulele – Some Basics

Before you can start playing your ukulele, you need to be able to read a chord chart. So let's take a look at how to do that. The typical chord chart is just a schematic of your fingerboard, looking on it as if you were holding your ukulele up in front of you, as shown in the figure on the right.

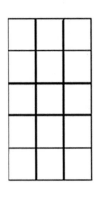 

The fingerboard is usually made of wood and it has thin metal strips across it, called 'frets'. You press down on the strings with your fingertips, in the spaces *between* these frets, to make the different notes and chords. Normal shorthand is to indicate finger placement above each fret. So, for example, if I was to tell you to *"place your finger on the 'first' fret"*, I would actually mean for you to place you finger in the space *above* the first fret.

Most of the chords for beginners use only the first few frets, and so the typical chord chart only shows part of the fingerboard. In the example above, the chord chart shows only the first five frets. On the actual ukulele, there is a dot to mark the location of the 5th fret (and the 7th, 10th,

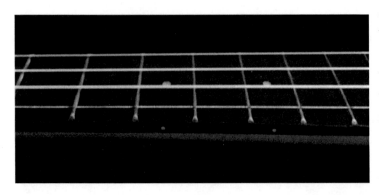

and 12th frets, as well). This helps you to position your fingers more quickly. Since it's not usually convenient to try to peer around to see the face of the fingerboard while you're playing, most ukuleles also have small dots along the top edge of the fingerboard at these same frets, as shown here in the photo on the left.

In addition to frets – the typical chord chart shows the four ukulele strings. We generally count them from right to left, as shown in the diagram here. The most common tuning on soprano, concert, and tenor ukuleles is as follows: G(4) C(3) E(2) and A(1). With 'low G tuning' the G (4th) string is a lower pitched note than all the others. However, most ukuleles you buy come with "reentrant tuning" in which this G (4th) string is an octave higher than that used in a low G tuning. Each type of tuning gives a slightly different sound and is useful for different types of playing. That's why

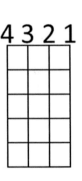

4 3 2 1

some people have two ukuleles – so they can have one with low G tuning and one with reentrant tuning. Personally, I prefer the low G tuning but reentrant tuning is far more common, so I suggest you start with that and try low G tuning later on when you get more experienced. Since the 4th string is always a G note (low or high) the chords do not change between the two. The baritone ukulele is the exception. Its strings are tuned like the first four strings of a guitar, so you'd use guitar chord charts for that type of ukulele. Since there are already tons of chord books out there for the guitar, I'll stick to the chord charts applicable to the smaller (soprano, concert, and tenor) ukuleles in this book.

On our chord charts, we use a black dot to indicate finger placement. We can also play a string open – that is, with no finger on any fret. We use a small 'o' above the string to signify that. In some cases, we might not want to play a particular string at all – in that case, we use a small 'x' above the string to denote that. Let's look at an example to illustrate this. For the chord chart on the right, you would

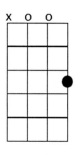

place a finger on the first string at the third fret, play the second and third strings open, and you would not play the fourth string at all. The photo beside the chord chart shows this on the actual ukulele. Note that you have to press down firmly with the tip of your finger to get a clear sound.

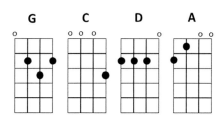

Here on the left are a few examples of common chords for the ukulele. (I've provided a comprehensive chord chart on page 24 of this book.) It's important to note that there are many different ways to play each chord; the ones shown in this book are the simplest versions that I could find of each. As you look at the ones with two or three black dots, you're

probably wondering which fingers to use where. Well, just as there are many different finger patterns for playing most chords, there are many different finger combinations you can use to make any particular version of a chord. Often you decide based on what's most comfortable for you, but you should also be thinking of what chords are coming next and how quickly you can get to them.

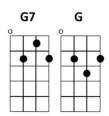

I find that the secret to being able to change chords quickly (aside from lots of practice) is to choose finger patterns that will help me to get into position for the next chord I will be playing. Using my pinky finger is usually a key aspect of this

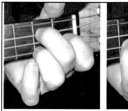

G7 chord (left) and G chord (right).

strategy. For example, consider the G7 and G chords – these often get played one after the other. If you keep your middle finger on the second fret of the third string and your ring finger on the second fret of the first string – you just have to put your index finger on the first fret of the second string to play a G7 chord. To change to a G chord, just add your pinky on the third fret of the second string. Then lift the pinky and you're back to G7 chord.

It's similar for the D7 and D chords, as shown in the photos below. If you put your middle finger on the second fret of the fourth string and your pinky finger on the second fret of the second string, you've got a D7 chord. Now just add 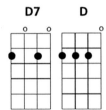 your ring finger on the second fret of the third string and, 'voila!' you've got a D chord. Lift the ring finger and you're back to

D7 chord (left) and D chord (right).

the D7. Note that for these photos, I have pulled my other fingers away to make it easier for you to see what I'm doing; however, when I'm playing, I actually keep all of my fingers curled over the fingerboard close to the strings, so that I'm ready to put them right back down when needed.

A friend commented recently that I don't seem to use my index finger all that much when I'm playing the ukulele and it's true; it's because I use my pinky finger a lot in the way I have just described. If you consciously try to use your pinky as much as possible, it can really help you to become quicker at changing chords. Think about this as well – I sometimes use different finger patterns for the same chord – depending upon which chord I will play next, or have just played. Don't constrain yourself to any particular pattern – learn to be flexible – and have that pinky in your arsenal to draw upon anytime!

Okay, well that gives you a bit of a start on how to read the chord charts and where to put the fingers of your left hand, but what about your right hand? What do you do to the strings to actually make music come out of this instrument? Well, you can pluck each string individually, you can strum them all, or you can do some combination of the two. For starters I suggest you just strum slowly and deliberately and practice this until you can get a melodious sound out of each string. If any of the strings sounds funny (non-musical), the first thing to check is that you're actually pressing down on the string hard enough at the fingerboard. Placing your finger a bit closer to the fret sometimes helps in getting a clearer sound, as well.

You can strum down with the side of your thumb for a harp-like sound (top right) or you can strum up and down with the tip of your index finger for a more mandolin-like sound (bottom right). Try both and see which works best for you – it will usually depend on the type of song you're playing – fast or slow. Later you can advance to more complex strum patterns like 'down-up-down' or 'down-down-up', or some variation that sounds and feels good to you for the particular song you're playing.

 As you get more experienced, you might like to try out some finger picking patterns. The simplest is to use your thumb to pluck string 4, and your index middle, and ring fingers to pluck strings 3, 2 and 1, respectively. Once you get comfortable with simple patterns like 4, 3, 2, 1 and 1, 2, 3, 4, you can try fancier ones, like 4, 1, 3, 2, or 4, 2, 3, 1. It also sometimes sounds nice to pick the 4th or 3rd string and then strum all four once or twice, depending upon whether the song is in 4/4 time (that is, it has a '1, 2, 3, 4' beat) or 3/4 time (has a '1, 2, 3' beat).

Some Final Tips for the Absolute Beginner

It was pretty easy for me to get going on the ukulele, since I'd been playing guitar for a long time. However, if you have never played any stringed instrument before, it helps to have a few tips to get you going as quickly as possible. Here are a few things I'd suggest for beginners.

Tip # 1 – cut your left hand's fingernails REALLY short!

To get a clean sound you need to press the strings with the very tips of your fingers and this means you need to cut your fingernails very short. If you can see more than a trace of white on the nail tip, then you're probably not cutting enough off.

Tip # 2 – put the chord charts right on the song sheets

This is how I learned all the chords I needed in just a few days – I took all the song sheets that we were using in the band and added the relevant ukulele chord diagrams right onto them. That way I could remind myself of all of the chords I needed for each song, without having to refer back to the chord chart all the time. You'll see examples of this in the song sheets I've provided for you at the back of this book.

Tip # 3 – use fingering exercises to gradually build up the calluses

One of the hardest parts of learning to play a stringed instrument is dealing with the pain in the tips of the fingers of your left hand (assuming you are playing your ukulele 'right handed'). After a while your fingertips will build up calluses for protection but, until then, playing will be a painful experience. I found two things helped me to deal with this. The first was to start off each session with some fingering exercises. Pluck the first string open, then with your index finger on the first fret, then with your middle finger on the second fret, then with your ring finger on the third fret, and finally with your pinky finger on the fourth fret. Do the pinky one twice and then work your way back down: ring finger on the third fret, middle finger on the second fret, index finger on the first fret, then open. Now move to the second string and repeat the pattern. Then do the third string and, finally, the fourth. Run through this a few times at the beginning of each practice. Not only will it toughen up your fingertips, it will limber up your fingers. You can also use this exercise to limber up your right hand, too – by using different fingers to pluck the strings as you go.

The second thing I found that helped in the early stages of toughening up the fingertips was to play for a short amount of time (for example, 10 to 15 minutes) several times a days, instead of playing for one long (60 to 90 minute) session. You need to play at least a bit every day to build up those calluses. So even if you only have time to run through those exercises a few times… do it! Your fingers will thank you.

Tip # 4 – start slow

No matter what finger patterns you eventually decide you prefer for the various chords – it will take time to get good at changing chords. The important thing to remember is to never sacrifice accuracy for speed. Otherwise you can develop some very bad habits that are hard to get rid of later on. Take it slow, make sure you get a nice clean sound with each chord, and ensure that you have your fingers correctly placed. Strum slowly and deliberately – get some volume out of your instrument. If it helps, start with slow songs and ones that don't have a lot of chord changes in them. That way you won't feel pressured to change chords quickly while you are learning. Let your skill evolve naturally. Eventually, as the muscle memories develop, finger placements and chord changes will become automatic – then you will find you can do them faster with no effort at all.

Tip # 5 – play along with others

There are tons of *YouTube* videos on playing the ukulele. You can play along with these and get the feel for rhythm and pace. And it sounds good because someone plays along with you! I also like to include the artist's names when I look up music online – so I can play along with their CDs or videos. First, I find the chords for the song I want to learn by using the following search string: "Guitar chords for *some song* by *some artist*", substituting the song title and performer I am interested in at the time. This usually leads me to the music in the key that they performed it in. Once I have the music, I look up the performance on *YouTube* and play along with their recording of the song. It's a great way to have fun learning new songs. (Note that I search for guitar music instead of for ukulele music simply because there are many more songs on-line for guitars than there are for ukuleles. With your ukulele chord chart in hand, you can use either.)

Also, play along with your friends whenever you can. You may have to remind them to slow down a bit from time to time but don't be shy to do it, they were once beginners too, so they'll be sympathetic. It will be a ton of fun for all of you and you'll learn much faster, so start doing that as soon as possible.

Christmas Tunes to Get You Started

Assuming you got your ukulele for Christmas, what better songs to get started with than the songs of the season? So in the following pages you will find an assortment of Christmas songs to play on your new ukulele. I've organized them so that you can try the easiest ones first and move on gradually to those with more chord changes and/or more challenging chords.

I suggest you take it slow to start with – just strum each chord deliberately. If you find the chord changes too quick, or if you cannot manage one, don't worry – you can just skip it, keep on singing, and resume playing with the next chord you know or can get to.

I hope you have fun!

Jingle Bells

James Lord Pierpont, 1857

CHORUS:

G

Jingle bells, jingle bells, jingle all the way.

C   G   A7   D7

Oh what fun it is to ride in a one horse open sleigh, Hey!

G

Jingle bells, jingle bells, jingle all the way,

C   G   D7   G

Oh what fun it is to ride in a one horse open sleigh.

VERSE 1:

G   C

Dashing through the snow, with a one horse open sleigh,

Am   D7   G

O'er the fields we go, laughing all the way,

                               C

Bells on bob-tail ring, making spirits bright,

      Am   G   D7   G   D7

What fun it is to ride and sing a sleighing song tonight. Oh!

CHORUS

VERSE 2:

G   C

A day or two ago, I thought I'd take a ride,

   Am   D7   G

And soon Miss Fannie Bright, was seated by my side;

                                      C

The horse was lean and lank; misfortune seemed his lot;

   Am   G   D7   G   D7

He fell into a drifted bank, and then we got upsot. Oh!

Jingle Bells – pg 2

VERSE 3:

G   C
Now the ground is white, so go it while you're young,
Am   D7   G
Take the girls tonight and sing this sleighing song;

                                                       C
Just get a bob-tailed bay two-forty as his speed
Am   G   D7   G   D7
Hitch him to an open sleigh and crack! you'll take the lead. Oh!

  G
Jingle bells, jingle bells, jingle all the way.
C   G   A7   D7
Oh what fun it is to ride in a one horse open sleigh, Hey!
  G
Jingle bells, jingle bells, jingle all the way,
C   G   D7   G
Oh what fun it is to ride in a one -----horse -----op---en ------sleigh.

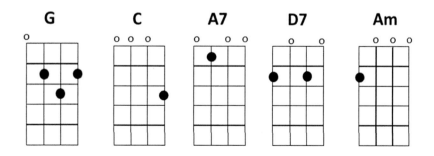

Silent Night

Father Josef Mohr, 1816

G
Silent night holy night
D7   G
All is calm, all is bright
C   G
Round yon virgin mother and child.
C   G
Holy infant so tender and mild,
D7   G   D7   G
Sleep in heavenly peace. Sleep in heavenly peace.

G
Silent night holy night
D7   G
Shepherds quake at the sight,
C   G
Glories stream from heaven afar,
C   G
Heavenly hosts sing alleluia;
D7   G   D7   G
Christ the Savior, is born. Christ the Savior, is born.

G
Silent night holy night
D7   G
Son of God, love's pure light
C   G
Radiant beams from thy holy face,
C   G
With the dawn of redeeming grace,
D7   G   D7   G
Jesus, Lord, at thy birth. Jesus, Lord, at thy birth.

16

O Come, All Ye Faithful

John Francis Wade, 1751

```
       G          D      G        C  G  D
O come, all ye faithful, joyful and tri-um-phant;
      Em  D         G       D    A     D
O come ye, O come ye to Beth- eth-le-hem.
G            D    G    D     Em      D
Come and behold Him, Born the King of angels.
       G                                    D
 O come, let us adore Him;  O come, let us  a--dore Him;
       Am          D    G     D      G
 O come, let us  a--dore Him, Chr-ist the Lord!

    G          D      G        C  G  D
Sing choirs of angels, sing in ex—ul—ta—tion;
    Em  D          G      D    A    D
O sing, all ye bri—ght hosts of hea--v'n a-bove.
G          D  G  D  Em      D
Glo-ry to God all, glory in the highest.
       G                                    D
 O come, let us adore Him;  O come, let us  a--dore Him;
       Am          D    G     D      G
 O come, let us  a--dore Him, Chr-ist the Lord!

  G          D        G          C  G    D
Yea Lord we greet Thee; born this hap--py morn--ing,
Em        D  G    D    A    D
Jesus, to Thee be all glo—ry   giv'n.
G          D  G   D     Em       D
Word of  the Father, now in flesh ap—pear—ing.
       G                                    D
 O come, let us adore Him;  O come, let us  a--dore Him;
       Am          D    G     D      G
 O come, let us  a--dore Him, Chr-ist the Lord!
```

G
D
C
Em
A
Am

17

God Rest Ye Merry, Gentlemen

Traditional, 15th Century

Em

C

B7

Am

G

D

     Em   **C**   **B7**
God rest ye merry, gentlemen, let nothing you dismay.
    Em   **C**   **B7**
Remember Christ our Savior, was born on Christmas Day.
    Am   **G**   **Em**   **D**
To save us all from Satan's pow'r, when we were gone astray.
  G   **B7**   **Em**   **D**
O tidings of comfort and joy, comfort and joy.
  G   **B7**   **Em**
O tidings of comfort and joy!

    Em   **C**   **B7**
In Bethlehem, in Israel, this blessed Babe was born.
    Em   **C**   **B7**
And laid within a manger upon this blessed morn.
    Am   **G**   **Em**   **D**
The which his Mother Mary did nothing take in scorn.
  G   **B7**   **Em**   **D**
O tidings of comfort and joy, comfort and joy.
  G   **B7**   **Em**
O tidings of comfort and joy!

    Em   **C**   **B7**
From God our heav'nly Father, a blessed angel came.
    Em   **C**   **B7**
And unto certain shepherds, brought tidings of the same.
    Am   **G**   **Em**   **D**
How that in Bethlehem was born the Son of God by name.
  G   **B7**   **Em**   **D**
O tidings of comfort and joy, comfort and joy.
  G   **B7**   **Em**
O tidings of comfort and joy!

Joy to the World

Issac Watts, 1719

```
D                    Em  D   A7   D       G       A         D
```
Joy to the world! The Lord has come; let earth re-ceive her King.
```
D            D
```
Let every heart, prepare Him room,
```
                              A7
```
And heav'n and nature sing, And heav'n and nature sing,
```
        D      G   D      Em  D  A7   D
```
And heav'n and heav'n and na-ture sing.

```
D                    Em  D  A7    D         G         A          D
```
Joy to the world! The Sa-vior reigns; let men their songs em-ploy.
```
            D
```
While fields and floods, rocks, hills and plains,
```
                            A7
```
Repeat the sounding joy, re-peat the sounding joy,
```
        D      G   D   Em     D     A7   D
```
Re-peat, re-peat the sound-ing joy.

```
D                    Em    D    A7   D        G         A         D
```
He rules the world with truth and grace; and makes the nations prove.
```
            D
```
The glories of His righteousness,
```
                          A7
```
And wonders of his love, and wonders of his love,
```
        D    G     D   Em   D   A7   D
```
And won-ders, won-ders of his love.

Hark the Herald Angels Sing

Lyrics: Charles Wesley, 1739, Music: Felix Mendelssohn, 1840

```
G       C      G      D    G    C    G    D   G
Hark the herald angels sing, "Glory to the new born King,
G            C      G      A    D      A     D   A    D
Peace on earth and mercy mild, God and sinners re-con-ciled"
G    D    C      D    G      D      C       D
Joyful all ye nations rise, join the triumph of the skies
C            Am              D     G     C    D  G
With angelic host proclaim, "Christ is born in Beth-le-hem"
C            Am              D     G     C    D  G
Hark the herald angels sing, "Glory to the new born King."
```

```
G          C      G      D       G       C    G    D  G
Christ, by highest heaven adored; Christ the ever-last-ing Lord;
G      C        G      A    D      A     D   A    D
Late in time behold him come, Offspring of the fa--vored one.
G         D         C       D   G        D      C   D
Veiled in flesh, the Godhead see; hail th'in-carnate Die--ty
C            Am              D     G           C    D  G
Pleased as man with men to dwell, Jesus, our Im--man--u--el
C            Am              D     G     C    D  G
Hark the herald angels sing, "Glory to the new born King"
```

```
G         C        G        D    G        C     G    D   G
Hail! the heav'n-born Prince of Peace. Hail the son of Righteousness
G         C      G      A    D        A     D  A     D
Light and life to all He brings, risen with healing in His wings
G       D       C     D  G       D       C          D
Mild He lays His glory by, born that man no more may die
C                Am           D      G         C    D  G
Born to raise the sons of earth, born to give them se--cond birth
C                Am           D      G     C    D  G
Hark the herald angels sing, "Glory to the new born King"
```

G

C

D

A

Am

20

The First Noel

Traditional, 13 to 14th Century

D

A

G

A7

```
D           A        D   G D
The first No- - el  the  angel did say,
G        D       A7    D                A7    D
Was to certain poor shepherds in fields as they lay;
A7 D           A        D       G       D
In fields where they lay keeping their sheep,
G     D                          A7  D
On a cold winter's night, that was so deep.
A7  D              G        D            G     D A7 D
No--el,  No---el, No--el,  No--el, born is the King of Is--ra--el.


D             A        D G D
They looked up and saw a star,
G      D A7   D                 A7    D
Shining in the East,    beyond them far;
A7   D       A        D      G      D
And to the earth it gave great light,
G    D                        A7    D
And so it continued both day and night.
A7  D              G        D            G     D A7 D
No--el,  No---el, No--el,  No--el, born is the King of Is--ra--el.


D               A        D G  D
This star drew nigh to  the northwest,
G     D  A7   D           A7 D
O'er Beth--le--hem, it took its rest;
A7   D       A         D    G   D
And there it did both stop and stay,
G     D                        A7 D
Right o'er the place where Jes-us lay.
A7  D              G        D            G     D A7 D
No--el,  No---el, No--el,  No--el, born is the King of Is--ra--el.
```

Deck the Halls

Traditional Welsh Carol, 16th Century

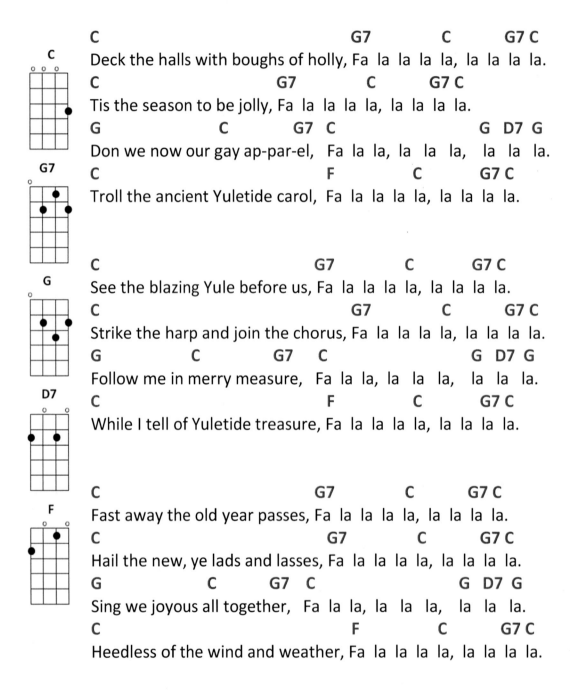

```
C                              G7        C        G7 C
Deck the halls with boughs of holly, Fa la la la la, la la la la.
C                        G7        C      G7 C
Tis the season to be jolly, Fa la la la la, la la la la.
G              C        G7  C                  G  D7 G
Don we now our gay ap-par-el,  Fa la la, la la la,  la la la.
C                          F          C        G7 C
Troll the ancient Yuletide carol,  Fa la la la la, la la la la.
```

```
C                              G7        C        G7 C
See the blazing Yule before us, Fa la la la la, la la la la.
C                              G7        C        G7 C
Strike the harp and join the chorus, Fa la la la la, la la la la.
G              C        G7  C                  G  D7 G
Follow me in merry measure,  Fa la la, la la la,  la la la.
C                          F          C        G7 C
While I tell of Yuletide treasure, Fa la la la la, la la la la.
```

```
C                              G7        C        G7 C
Fast away the old year passes, Fa la la la la, la la la la.
C                              G7        C        G7 C
Hail the new, ye lads and lasses, Fa la la la la, la la la la.
G              C        G7  C                  G  D7 G
Sing we joyous all together,  Fa la la, la la la,  la la la.
C                              F          C        G7 C
Heedless of the wind and weather, Fa la la la la, la la la la.
```

We Wish You a Merry Christmas

Traditional

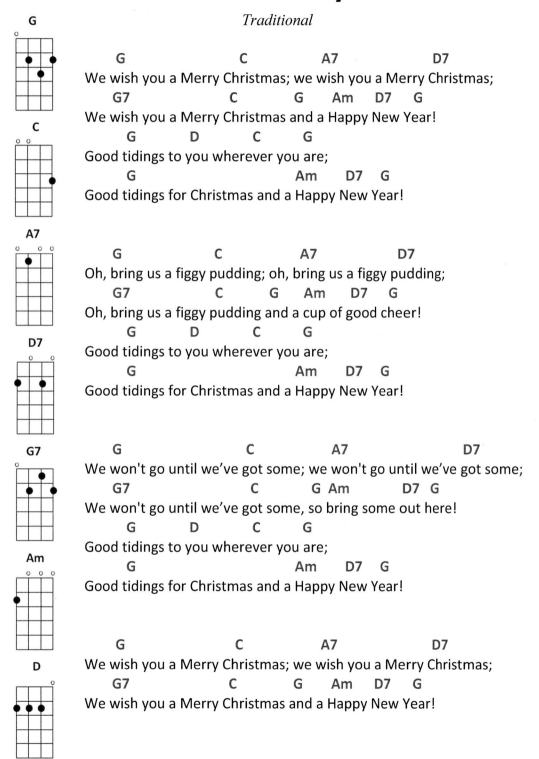

G (chord diagram)

C (chord diagram)

A7 (chord diagram)

D7 (chord diagram)

G7 (chord diagram)

Am (chord diagram)

D (chord diagram)

G	C	A7	D7

We wish you a Merry Christmas; we wish you a Merry Christmas;

| G7 | C | G | Am | D7 | G |
We wish you a Merry Christmas and a Happy New Year!

| G | D | C | G |
Good tidings to you wherever you are;

| G | | Am | D7 | G |
Good tidings for Christmas and a Happy New Year!

| G | C | A7 | D7 |
Oh, bring us a figgy pudding; oh, bring us a figgy pudding;

| G7 | C | G | Am | D7 | G |
Oh, bring us a figgy pudding and a cup of good cheer!

| G | D | C | G |
Good tidings to you wherever you are;

| G | | Am | D7 | G |
Good tidings for Christmas and a Happy New Year!

| G | C | A7 | D7 |
We won't go until we've got some; we won't go until we've got some;

| G7 | C | G Am | D7 G |
We won't go until we've got some, so bring some out here!

| G | D | C | G |
Good tidings to you wherever you are;

| G | | Am | D7 | G |
Good tidings for Christmas and a Happy New Year!

| G | C | A7 | D7 |
We wish you a Merry Christmas; we wish you a Merry Christmas;

| G7 | C | G | Am | D7 | G |
We wish you a Merry Christmas and a Happy New Year!

Ukulele Chord Chart

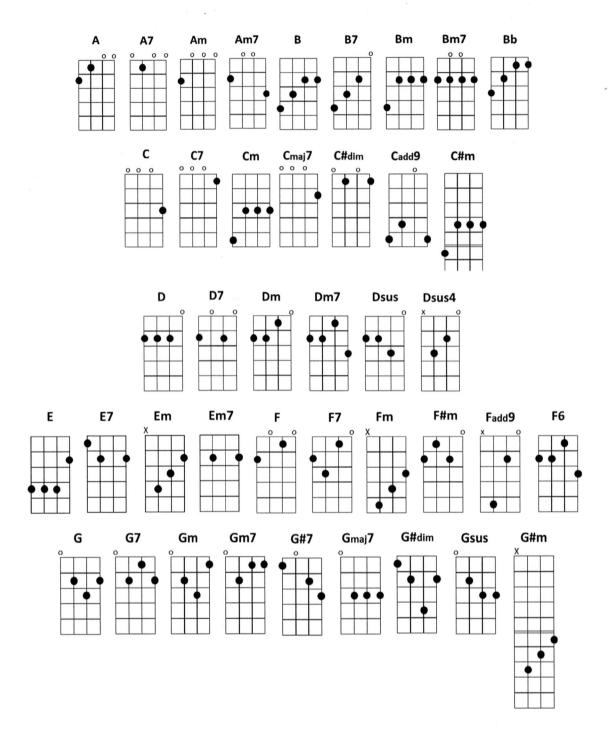

ABOUT THE AUTHOR – FAYE HICKS

Faye is a Canadian writer and a retired engineering professor. She lives in eastern Canada (New Brunswick) with her husband, Les, and their furry family of rescued cats and dogs. Faye plays the guitar, ukulele and bodhran – and is also a keen student of fiddle and mandolin. She and Les play in a band that entertains local seniors.

Faye enjoys writing both fiction and creative non-fiction. She has written one novel, Defining Moments, two humorous short story collections: A Day in the Life of a Professor and Who Says You Can't Herd Cats? as well as a number of technical books. All are available as eBooks and paperback on Amazon.com and affiliates. Faye is currently working on her second novel and also blogs at fayehicks.wordpress.com. For links to her writing and for more info, please check out her website at www.fayehicks.com.

Made in the USA
San Bernardino, CA
07 December 2016